JN440340

Love Songs Sung with the Body

Love Songs Sung with the Body

A collection of new poems by Kim Byung-ho
Translated by Brother Anthony of Taizé

K POET

아시아

Contents

LOVE SONGS SUNG WITH THE BODY

Spell for the left hand

1.

Neither he nor the rough hand that slapped him could have imagined that the spell he had recited would come back as a slap.

A spell is like an order of things that will disappear. His voice trembled openly as the woman found traces of her own name passing within the spell.

He had insisted that the spell should have no meaning, but there was no meaning to his life.

The fact that meaning is like a spell in living was something he realized on the day of the harsh slap he received from his left hand.

While he was piecing together the words of his

protest, he realized it too late and stood at the entrance to the alley, a shadow growing longer in late autumn.

2.

The woman's left hand was rough, harsh, and dry. Her right hand was very considerate and knew how to caress wounds. Above all, it was soft. That day was Left Hand Day. His hand, which was roughly grasping her, shook her neck violently and did not let go.

Love is left handed. He loved like a boat fluttering in a typhoon.

It took six rounds of reheating to get his

words out. The grains of rice that sank like that became a spell.

The meaning is the trajectory of rice grains that were shaken cruelly. No one remembers,

but at some point in his love, he vomitted a spell.

Bipungchodongpalsam*

So the fight is for the right hand.

3.

There was no need for order in throwing things away.

If abandoning things in that order and remaining was the meaning, it was something

that could be survived by overcoming them.
Even footprints that were less wet during rainy autumn nights could be found.
It was a good idea to at least try to make love. It was a head that could have been gently torn off and passed over.
So he sang with the sound of a whale.
Bipungchodongpalsam
If there is an order to things that disappear, when all that remains is to live,
an excuse to breathe, in which grave were you buried?
Where was the woman's name buried in the spell?

I couldn't ask.

4.

A hug is like squeezing the wind out of the lungs. My ears cried as the wind passed by, and it eventually became a whistle in his eyes. When the woman turned around, it was Left Hand Day again. Bipungchodongpalsam

* In the Korean card game *Hwatu*, this is a customary spell recited when a player has to give up their cards because they have nothing they can use. It can be said to be the reverse of things considered to be of great value, the order in which things that need to be discarded are placed.

Mobius money

He twisted one end of the money one hundred and eighty degrees and joined it to the other end. He wanted to make endless money, but it just went in and out endlessly, and if there was an end, it wasn't even money. It took a full twenty-four hours to set off during the day, when the shadows were shortest, and follow the money around once. He set off after King Sejong, but when he returned, the armillary sphere greeted him, and the night was curled up where the day had been, so instead of a dream, reality was fierce.

I would leave in the middle of the night, walk another day, and when I returned home, I would find Shin Saimdang with jaundice frowning in the clean yard at noon. When asked why the faces of people without money and debts were depicted on the face of money, he said that if you borrow money as if in a dream, you can see what is written on the back of money, just as you cannot hear the sound of a ventilator purring when you apply strength to your lower abdomen. When I turned around and sat back down in the world with my back to me, my lower abdomen tightened as I couldn't hear the sound of a ventilator. As the hours of indigestion poured out from exhaustion, salmonella bacteria grew in my stomach. Even if it made no sense, it wasn't about money.

All-purpose condom

—Mobius Money 2

It wasn't about making it possible with anyone, it was about making it possible with anything. Although he did not know it, not being able to read between the lines of the stars was also a sin of the times.

The moment you put it on, you could become physically entangled with not only rhinos, but bats, and even poppies fluttering in the fields.

—What does the identity of the other person matter? The seams of my desire burst open and new shoots sprout,

One day, he recalled his relationship with a 500-year-old pine tree.

—He was deep, wise, and knew how to feel very slowly. Above all, he had a deep scent fermented by time, but breaking away from the over-concentrated stickiness of time was arduous and arduous. For me, he was too long, and for him, I was too short. However, because it was a tragedy,

Although this experience was personal and could not be confirmed, everyone knew the news that the next day, an old pine tree that had protected the ancient temple for a thousand years had withered and died for no reason.

This unexpectedly became a medium that opened the way for crossbreeding between different species and opened up a new market, but as a side effect, it caused a plague of the mind without a vaccine. Afterwards, while looking for a simpler method, the villagers called what was created money. There were some who said that this was also the work of dark forces, but a rumor spread through the village that even physical entanglement was the excrement of a world that tried to overcome all forms of barriers.

Dirty woman

There are more reasons why a woman dumps a man than bubbling air bubbles.

Of course, the unpleasant smell was the problem with the hot breath of this late spring day.

In a season of oversaturated moisture and sweat, it turns into a distant asteroid, wandering around a distorted elliptical orbit with the woman as its focus but unable to approach.

The sound of falling leaves is sharp, times when love is broken, even if I cover my ears and endure it alone,

On a heavy snowy night, in the warm embrace of the blanket, the level of heat in the two bodies did not match.

The deepest wound for a man with a deep heart is

being told: I just got cleaned up so get away.

For others, washing one's body was for the next task, but for women, it was a final act like a period.

As far as a man knows,

I was struck hard by the realization that it only worked with the filthiest of women who appeared at every moment.

I came down the mountain along the path between the two paired peaks.

What is dirty is low, and what is low is

the floor that supports the world, it was the home of exhalation.

Sadness also collects on the floor and nowhere else.

It's a pity that it's pooling in my cold body.

What's inside me that's not mine

I was pounding nails into the wall with my butt while enduring the pain. Through the gaps in the pain, I could see the buttocks of an unknown woman in front of me. I gritted my teeth and asked what she was doing. She said she was nailing the wall with her ass.

I am the wall. I am the wall that is being nailed while enduring the pain of being stabbed, and I am the wall that is driving nails in without knowing that it is being stabbed. The pain that cannot be pulled out is used as a hammer, and the buttocks that cannot properly drive a single nail are a part of me, and a desire that glows without intention, an amorphous lava that is inside me but was not sown by me, is dragging me around. So I am a wall that is convulsing, and so the wall is a peaceful history. This is nonsense that has been passed down from our very ancient ancestors.

A host's love

It was a parking lot on top of an embankment attached to a small temple. The moonlight piled up like snow on the woman's head, and her fingers were thin and thin, unable to cover up the smile on her mouth.

The woman had brought out the car under the pretext of teaching him how to drive, but the car she gave the man was a cocoon where he could hide in reality and be left alone with the woman. Even when the car roared clumsily, the woman laughed, and even when its wheels miserably crossed the line, she giggled. The sound of laughter was enough to erase the image of his wife comforting her child from the man's eyes. The man's hot body temperature grazing her wrist overwhelmed the formal voice of her husband that dripped from the receiver every day.

That was all there was to the world at that time.

The children grew up and had other children. Years like moonlight had accumulated on the woman's head, but her fingers were still thin. When I met her again as her boss, she was a woman. She didn't try to erase her memories, and she didn't even pretend to know. But today, when she meets her old friend, she feels profane and profane.

The shirt of the woman who was moving away was a sheet of paper fluttering and sinking into the darkness. She was sad, but she wasn't sad. This too was a section of life.

His wife quietly argued with the man. The man informed the woman, and she did not reproach her husband so much. However, the secret link connecting the two families quietly revealed itself. The origin of the sexualized disease was the woman's husband, and the path was revealed by the man's wife. Such was the disturbance of the evil spirit, jealous of a man's love.

For a pathogen, it is good for the host's love to be broad rather than deep.

Uses of the ring finger

Some people think that the little finger still has a role to play in making a promise.
The use of the ring finger must have always flowed freely like a passing wind.
I erase the little eye mucus from last night
If even a single tear falls, it is removed quietly without anyone noticing,
The ring finger bowed its head and said to itself that it was sorry.
When closing the sliding door behind your back
it says its job is to press quietly without leaving any gap.
No one knows, but it's closing my heart so

tightly it doesn't leak,

it's done without anyone knowing, the wounded ring finger tingles, whispering in the morning.

Proving is a dog's thing

1.

A dog grazes next to a cow, and a farmer grazes next to it. They graze grass, but some eat it, some spit it out, and some kill it. This world, which is composed of properties where different results are revealed by changing the subject, goes beyond the problem of language and is a metaphor for the fact that not all life is a consistent action directed toward one goal. The dog proves this by munching on grass, and when he gets caught munching on a passing rabbit, he protests that it was a joke. However, some grazing behavior is not a joke.

2.

Nowadays, dogs have to struggle to drag people on leashes, so you can only meet dogs passing by in old fields across the river, carrying solitude all alone. A passing dog cannot smile.

The dog always passed first. On days when Chilseong's father stayed up all night at his parents' house without a phone call, a pot would tumble around in the narrow yard, shouting, 'Oh my gosh, I'm dying!', and before Seungja's mother could look through the wall to see what the neighbors were up to, a dog would check out the house first. It has passed.

If someone was to run down an alley, it was up

to the passing dog to establish the full story of the incident, what was the cause of the running, and at which end of the alley it ended with the person scratching the back of his or her head. Later, even when the love affair between Chilseong and Seungja was burning, it also enjoyed going around the backwaters of the neighborhood. It is the job of a passing dog to look into the distance and cry for a long time to protect the times when the paths of two youths collided so passionately from intruders.

The dog laughs. The dog laughs as it passes, as if it's a cool signal that nothing can be hotter than a prank.

3.

Some dogs pull carts and collect objects that have lost their meaning. The tonic that is customarily given is that of a dog, and the sticky attachments that the ex-boyfriend cannot let go of are contained in an invisible cart pulled by the dog. If you hand the dog a wad of money that you don't want to repay or a tasteless dish that was rejected and don't recite the mantra 'Give it to the dog,' you will have to spit out all the comfort the dog has given you over a long period of time, and finally, you will have to generously give your old habits to the dog.

They will become dog poop and become the medicine of the world,

Love that cannot come true

'When the human species chose to ensure genetic diversity in offspring by combining the two genders, female and male, there were inevitable fatal side effects, and the various mental side effects that appear in humans are collectively called love.' The argument was that of the presenter. Next, there was someone who narrowly expanded love to 'the common name for the act of creating descendants.' This was a materialistic perspective that reversed the subject and object and circumvented the previous definition.

The difference in perspectives was clearly evident in defining 'impossible love.' Those who supported the second definition argued that a horse and a donkey are a love that 'can be achieved.' This is because they produce offspring called mules. However, the mule becomes the tragic protagonist of an unfulfilled love that cannot produce descendants with anyone, and is so discouraged that it dies carrying only human burdens. When criticism arose that this was an overly human-centered thinking and a speculation that ignored the psychological side effects of love, a new claim was made that 'A poppy and a cat may be in love, but cannot be in a relationship.'

Those who were angry asked, 'So does this

mean that the song Yang Hee-eun sang is about establishing a genetically impossible relationship?' In addition, it is a base prejudice that excludes relationships between people with diseases related to fertility or same-sex couples from the category of love, and therefore, 'love that cannot be achieved' is justified by adding the factor of fate to the excuses found in the process of breaking up due to a change of heart. 'It's just a collection of hypocrisy,' he said.

The opponents again asked, 'Then what is true love?' and an impatient person shouted 'Marriage!' and was met with as much harshness as could be expected. 'Then what about divorce?

Is it a love that has been achieved but is lost again? Or is it an ignorant love that only realized after marriage that it could not be achieved? In the case of polyandry or polygamy, when the number of spouses is N, is love only achieved in proportion to 1/N?', the person being attacked held his hair and shouted eternally, 'Then what is fulfilled love again?' and someone else ended up saying something they really shouldn't have said. 'Seeds of tears!' All discussions end up in chaos. 'Think, man! So is tear gas also love?' 'Is yawning love?' and 'What else is not?'

After a long pause, the sage, returning from a long shit, put the crowd in order. "Since everything is a process, love may also be a process, and therefore, there is no love that is achieved, but love is something that comes to fruition..” But the unintentionally spittle-filled remark became a long spark thrown into the cooling oil. ‘If love is a process, does it follow that love changes? ‘If love is a process, does love naturally change? Isn’t love what doesn’t change? So where does love go? Where is its destination and what should the result be?’ Then someone muttered, but everyone could hear. ‘It’s all a joke when you don’t know your identity, have no destination, and have no right to do anything. It’s a joke. There is no mischief like love.’ So in the end, love, love that cannot come true,

Reincarnation

As soon as she puts down the spoon, she naturally lies down and picks up her phone, the princess. Lie face down, lie on your back, lie on your left side, lie on your right side, curl up, look up, look far away, look in front of your nose, put your hands down, this is the most diverse posture since Ssamboobba, the famous yogi who once commanded the Himalayas, the princess.

The butler recalls his old mother's will. 'If you lie down right after eating, you'll become a cow.' So what type of cow will you be? The princess. So what are the variables that determine the types of Korean beef, black beef, water buffalo, bison, and cattle? How does the species of cow change depending on the amount and type of meal, the time it takes to lie down after eating, and the lying posture? Since she is a princess, will she be a cow lying around freely somewhere in India, where cows are revered? Could a cow that ate so much grass and lie down on its back become a human being? Are there threats among cows saying, 'If you do that, you will become a human being!'? So, when the princess turns into a cow, can the cow, which was unable to learn its own habits, return to being a human by being as lazy as it likes? The princess. At that moment, there is a sound that resonates throughout the house. 'Moo'

According to inside-out panties

When she saw my panties inside out, the lady asked me, "Did something happen with your wife at home?" What I told my wife

when she said "disgusting" was because she saw my inside-out panties and whispered, "Is there anything else I can turn inside out besides my pants?" But

I stopped trying to turn over my poor pride, and made a fuss, so my inside-out panties ended up happening. With pitiful eyes, she asked me

if I knew the criteria for deciding what's the inside and outside of dust, and when my wife glared at my inside-out panties and asked if I didn't know that the inside was the side where

the shaking happened,
my instinct was to say, “That’s the moment when inside and outside turn inside out.” Even my upside-down reason realized
that it was the Big Bang that gave birth to the universe, but the countless events that fill our universe turned out to be just shabby seeds rattling around inside the dust,
so it was all due to my inside-out panties that led to an irreversible expansion.
My wife, seeing my inside-out panties, testified to the possibility of a universe where, if the washing machine is turned inside-out they can be washed without putting them in.

After I turned my panties inside out once more, random events quietly suffocated in the dust, and the quiet sleep I had without panties turned the day inside out and it became an eternity.

But they

It was 3:55 pm on a foggy Friday. Three men wearing black masks entered the Baekseong Bank in Soheung-dong as if a shadow had passed, locked the front door like a father guarding a child's sleep, and dispersed to their respective destinations lighter than a cat. They were holding rifles that might have been real, but the weapon that overpowered everyone was a static weapon of unknown weight. The security guard threw the gas gun in the trash can with a look of fear in his eyes, and the branch manager handed over the keys and a note with the safe's password clearly written down with both hands, fearing that he might misunderstand. The attendants inside the reception area waved their white palms at the men to show that they had not set off any alarms and started to back away, while the remaining customers willingly lay down on the cold floor. Instead of lying face-down, I lay down on my back. It was the posture of thirsty males waiting for their lover. None of the thousands of people passing the wall noticed this tyranny of silence. It was 4pm on a foggy Friday afternoon.

At 4:05 pm on Friday, when the fog evaporated, the men evaporated. Those who saw their last glimpses said that their masks had turned into rainbow colors and that they even had halos. The police, who rushed in like snorting bison, could not find a single missing coin or even a single scratch on anyone. Those who had entered and trampled on their political opponents mercilessly could not understand anything.

But everyone who was weighed down by the emptiness of that day knew. What did the men steal?

The young employees who had worked hard to join the company no longer dreamed of their future, the branch manager who was about to retire did not care about older customers, and the music that played softly from the entrance hall began to blame itself for being noisy. The smile faded from the grandmother's face as she looked at her young grandson. The lovers did not wait for each other, and the children who were running here and there, annoying the security guard, lost focus and only looked into the distance. This happened at the same time as the horses that were racing in the large picture on the wall relaxed their muscles and collapsed.

A lazy man's love

1.

Until onesome points out that they are subject to a bad spirit due to an identinc somewhere, the love that has already been used must be left in its alfin, melted place. If you return it to its alorigin place, life starts again from the beginning. With pain.

2.

Pain is the glue that attaches the mind to ityreal, or it is a blinder that blocks the sideout of reality. Since you can only see what is in front of you, you try to love when it hurts, and causebe you are bored and meaningless because you notcan make eye contact with meaninglessness, you try to love and die only because it is meaningless.

3.

So, when the wind blows in the shade, even the owshad in the shade disappears.

(Some words have the letters reversed and are similar to anagrams.)

Death of a lazy person

1.

A person who puts off even accepting the fact that the problem of death cannot be solved by postponing death is deceived into thinking that there is something to do before death, so he tries to ponepost death, and so he covers up death with empty stories, as if he were covering up love, even giving up life just to love,

2.

Death will come. The reason it is a human venintion is because everyone has been dying steadily, not because they created something new, but because they found a new function there. It was a stimulant that encouraged life, and then it was a hallucinogenic drug that twisted the ingceil, and the next moment it scared the living things. Because it was a lethal weapon that saved lives

3.

When even the way to surrender to death is blocked, death becomes just a burden on my shoulders, puts a stick called pairdes in my hand, and as I go around in circles on an empty day, even the reason for not being there disappears, so I just sit there.

4.

At some point, the air that flows in and out of my body will follow me around, but that's why I'm so lazy that I can't let anything fereinter with death, so I shake off the money like I'm dusting, and I don't stand up and I'm not afraid of love, so I don't have to die, and I don't know where to go as much as the dust that has been shaken off

5.

Suddenly waking up at dawn, cutting off nose hair, cutting flesh, nosebleeds that started outside the nose become a river that drains life and portsups the jungle, but as if this dawn had no particular reason, just as this dawn has no particular reason, I am bored with watering death, heating up the ecosystem and making it bubble with green. I have nowhere to go, but if I look closely, I am at the end of an obvious road with no sign..

(Some words have the letters reversed and are similar to anagrams.)

Self-potrait of a shadow

If you come to your senses, you will get hit a few times. So, when you grow up, you will become young, and rainwater must accumulate up to your ankles for dark clouds to gather and perhaps because of this, he drank more to reduce his health, lost muscles in his lower body to lose water from love, and gained belly fat because he was too comfortable cutting his toenails.

In a dirt field under the sticky spring sunlight, one, no, two cats are nestled under the driver's door of his old car, snuggling together. Unwilling to disturb them, he walked home, holding a long-haired green onion and a bruised apple in both hands. The deep spring shadow walked ahead so that no one would be warm.

So you to want do? I'm a shadow of you, minus the thickness of desire. So you to want do? The hard part was hard. Ha? Old love is a bitch, and when the wind whistles through memories, the shadow lies down. Ha! I thought it was gone, but it was a line of pain that made my stomach turn. Right! Cross the bridge in that shape every time.

There was no one at home, so perhaps there was no need to say no one was there.

A burn incident that occurred only once in the history of the neighborhood.

The screams were low-pitched. The screams turned into long sighs. It was in front of the gym shower. Of course he was naked.

As he entered the shower room, his eyes were caught by the writing on the soap bottle. Shower mate, and a shower in English is a person who puts on a show. So, thanks to the idea that a shower is always a show with someone watching, he may have turned the water tap carelessly.

He got his dick, especially its precious head, burned by the hot water that unexpectedly poured out of the shower. The pain that overtook the man was unprecedented in human history. The area where many nerves were concentrated, the part of the body that was the vanguard of pleasure, erupted into an active volcano of unbearable pain. The actual boss, the health trainer's mother, was alone at the counter, but he couldn't argue with her and headed to the pharmacy. His butt eas pushed back, a posture that humans went through a long time ago in an evolutionary process.

As three days passed, the woman's suspicions turned into questions and became reality. It was a natural result of the immature behavior of a man who stalked women a couple of times a week even though he was over 50. The answer from the man with the gray skin was embarrassing to believe and incredibly lame.

The reason is unknown, but the woman went to the man's favorite bar (which the man believed was a complete secret) and knocked over two of the tables, but was kicked out without being able to grab the female manager's hair. Thanks to this, the man found out that the female manager was a judo athlete who used to fly in a small county. Instead of the man she couldn't contact, the excited female manager found Kwon, the bad real estate owner who had been visiting the bar with her, and poured out a stern protest, ending with an abstract warning. President Kwon conveyed this unexpected lightning strike to the technician who was fixing the boiler in the kitchen. Both of their eyes started to turn red as they started pouring out floating salty words like it took a long time, it was expensive, it was frequent. Although he came out saying that he was like a 30-year-old boiler whose parts were difficult to find, the boiler technician opened the door to the next repair location, a gym, without being able to remove the evil spirit from his back.

The daytime gym was an old cave. The problem with the boiler was with the valve that mixed hot and cold water, but it was minor.

There was some hot water left in the repaired boiler, and the moment he was about to open the cold water valve to neutralize it, someone turned on the water in the shower room. In a very short moment, water like unhardened lava escaped, and a single, low-pitched scream floated around as an echo inside the ancient cave and turned into a sigh.

Three syllogisms that speak of the world

1.

Desire is the engine that endures meaninglessness and drives the body to the end of life.

Senses are the fuel that activates desire and makes it run wild.

Therefore, without the body, there is no desire and meaninglessness disappears, but the surviving body completes the miserable reality through desire.

2.

The countless overlapping, tangled, festering juices of desire are called misfortune.

It is ignorance of the world that completes

the process in which desires fail to ferment and fester.

Therefore, by lumping together all the things that are not happiness, we have no choice but to call them unhappiness. This is because no one has the ability to look into every nook and cranny of that vast land where pus flows, and before that, no one knows what happiness is.

3.

If mass is existence, then weight is existence.

Melancholy is the distance between the world and events. It is a measure of distance.

Therefore, the masses hanging in space and

time are events, and the weight aligns the events so that they point in one direction, which is the direction of depression.

A contradiction called contradiction

It is easy to be so intoxicated with the satisfaction of being alive that one does not notice that living is essentially unrelated to meaning. In other words, (this is the hidden basic principle of a successful life in the human species), there is a gap between life and meaning. This means that one is blinded by the illusion that there is some kind of relationship with the world and cannot see the fundamental contradiction that the purpose of living is simply living.

The fact that it is not something to live for if you can get the hang of it is in the same vein as proving that it is not even a desire if there is an appropriate reason. The person who asked the pinwheel, wondering why it was spinning, why it was spinning, and why it had to turn, 'Did you spin?' was a crazy wind that did not know why it was blowing, why it was blowing, or why it had to blow.

Rebellious force

—World theory joke

A middle school boy whose only knowledge is rebellion mutters while taking off his clothes in the bathroom.

—I don't know the meaning of living,

A middle-aged guy who lived like that 30 years ago looks in the mirror and grumbles.

—Why? If I knew, I'd stop living, right? I'm still alive because I don't know that, man.

Even though the Earth pulls the hydrogen balloon, it resists and moves away. There is probably a place somewhere in the sky where balloons gather and live. These ignorant balloons have nothing to rebel against, so they just live together.

Twenty questions

Where do I put my shoes?

When did you pass the door?

How long is that darkness?

How deep was the withering time there?

How did the ooze that melted in the sun last fall curl up?

What color does the sigh taken from me fly in?

Where do the wet folds of darkness flow?

The space there is so distorted that the line called you blinks.

Is there a place to disappear?

So at what time was the point called you taken?

What horizon do I have to hang on to before I

can return?
How does time slope from hand to toe?
How many pieces will it tear into?
Can we reach the bottom?
Can you blink?
Where should I hang it? The time you were stamped,
can I fix it on time?
Will it disappear completely?
Can't you look back from somewhere?
Where did I put my shoes?

POET´S NOTE

It's not that far,
it's not a particularly difficult road,
Is there any problem?
If you just go along huffing and puffing, it'll be fine

My deceased mother, coming into my dreams, smiles and recovers.

POET´S ESSAY

The logic of the joke

Two old men were under the roof of a bus stop in the July sun, one standing, one sitting. The one seated, well into his eighties, speaks to the old man standing, who appears to be well into his mid-eighties.

"Did you hear or not? Youngchil's younger brother. Well, he died not long ago."

"Die? Why did he die? How old was he?"

"Maybe seventy-six? About that."

"Why did such a young guy die?"

"I don't know, seeing the hospital reminded me of him."

"He died because he was lazy. If we can breathe easily like this, why die? He died because he was lazy."

Someone cleans up the hidden waterway through which life flows. As long as you breathe well, you live. So, as long as you are not lazy in managing your breath, you will live well. This sharp Occam's razor sends shivers down the spine of anyone who hears it.

This is what science does. I will try to find the principles behind how the world moves and summarize them simply. Things with mass just pull on each other. It is the principle by which our universe operates. There are two types of electricity; if they are different, they pull, and if they are the same, they push. It is the principle by which our beings maintain their form. There are many more complicated principles, but let's just leave it to science. Because that's what it does.

Poetry also does this. It is about tracing the principles of emotion. If you trace it and look into its inner story, you will find that it is usually the principle of sorrow. This principle has two backgrounds. It's the regret that comes from wanting to do something but not being able to do it, and the fate of having to do it even though you don't want to do it.

I want to love, I want to hug, I want to be together, I want to be together and look at the same place, but it doesn't work out. It seems to work but it doesn't, it seems to work but it doesn't work. It's not just an erotic relationship. The appearance of thirst among people is almost similar. In this way, the emotional reaction that occurs to us when we encounter an unbridgeable gap between life and desire is sorrow. Most poems are wandering lost somewhere.

Another thing is when you don't want to do something, but you have to do it. All within this class are children of death. People meet randomly without any choice, but once they know each other a little, they are forced to break up. Since we are mortal beings, we must separate and then look straight at the death that approaches us. We call this attitude of waiting for one's share of death destiny. How could it not be sad? The home of sorrow is right here.

The principle of sorrow that I have worked so hard to follow is a senseless evil that runs rampant between desire and death. But what? What do you know about that? So, are you telling me to live like green onion kimchi pickled in sorrow? Or, now that I have figured out the principle of sorrow, will I die writing a heavily salted poem? After hearing this question and answer, the old man at the bus stop will pick up the same sharpened razor blade.

"You are doing ridiculous things like going into the middle of a rice field and cutting all the rice with a lawn mower. I just need to take a deep breath and enjoy myself. Then if you die, so what?"

This is the logic of the joke. A joke is an experiment. It is an experiment that does not harm others, but causes scars in people's lives. What should I do if I don't do that? Can I do it?

COMMENTARY

The Physics of Love and Laughter

Ham Giseok (Poet)

Poetry and science are strange lovers. The methods of realizing beauty are different, and the procedures for finding the principles are also quite different. However, they are similar in that they long for the secrets of nature and the universe. The poet is the one who translates and interprets the unfamiliar love that passes between these two. The substances that make up the world move regularly according to physical principles, but the phenomena and aesthetics that this movement produces are variable and irregular, like love. Therefore, the beauty of this world must always be reinterpreted, newly translated, and interpreted. Kim Byung-ho is a unique poet who has continued this kind of love brokerage. He has released another book into the world. It is a story of observation of a fallen world and a story of the drift of love. It is a critical satire and enjoyable comedy directed at modern society in that it diagnoses and reflects on the inside and outside of our society by observing facts and events in the physical world.

In the material world, matter is energy, and energy circulates to sustain the world. In the human world, love serves as the energy. However, in the corrupt reality, love is corrupted into a substance subordinated to capital. To the poet, modern society is a world of tragic calculations where 'desire + sensation' becomes 'misfortune.' If we compare humans physically, they would be like creatures where 'mass is existence and weight is real,' and the poet explores the world of realistic weight where gravity operates rather than the world of theoretical mass. This means that his poetry focuses on the body rather than the mind. This means that the issues of desire and capital are approached from the perspective of reality rather than ideology.

He is a crooked sect. By looking at a character in a specific situation with a distorted gaze, he draws facts and psychology. He stumbles, laughs, and plays pranks, then makes use of a martial arts technique that strikes the opponent's vital points all at once. It is a kind of verbal drunkenness and humorous wild sword dance. The important body part at this time is the left hand. The left hand is the body that opposes the meaning-centered worldview, and in that it is a tool of rebellion against the existing old world, the left hand's day is the beginning of provocation and counterattack, and the time of love. His love unfolds in a way that overturns clichés by making fun of them, and in a way that rejects the expected narrative. It takes a method of paradox and irony, twisting the story as if to crush it and producing unexpected results. There are roughly three themes that are revealed through this. The first is a satire of social conditions and a caricature of late-capitalist society through sex-related materials, the second is reflection on human thought and criticism of rational worldviews using materials representing the mathematical world of logic, and the third is through symbol play and verbal play. It is an expression of subversive consciousness.

A characteristic material that reflects the poet's cynical perception of reality is condom panties. The all-purpose condom, a proxy for corrupt desires, is a distorted mirror image of our reality. The object of sex is expanded to an unlimited extent and sexual intercourse is carried out with all objects in the world. At this time, the subjectivity of the sexual partner is obliterated and the excretion of the condom user's desires becomes important. Therefore, this all-purpose condom is not a tool for loving communication, but is optimal for crossbreeding. It is a means of

In the case of panties, the event of turning the panties inside and out is treated as an important event comparable to the Big Bang, the birth of the universe. The fun thing about looking at the falsehood and evil of the world with an inverted reason by overturning the reason called panties is that many events in the world will ultimately be born from the hidden genitals inside the turned over panties. The dictatorial violence of rationality is ridiculed by caricaturing it as the genitals. In the end, the act of turning back the turned-over panties is the poet's will to overthrow the world of overturned acts and reduce it to the world of events of omission. The reverse idea of perversely inverting a distorted world through the language of humor is fun and refreshing.

"Mobius's Money" is a poem that humorously depicts the evil and horror of a capitalist society in which physical capital completely dominates and manipulates humans. A Möbius strip made by twisting banknotes through 180 degrees and sticking them together, the inside and outside disappearing, spins and turns endlessly, humorously depicting modern people unable to escape the bondage of money. The image of the narrator, unable to escape the bondage of money and boiling inside, is a portrait of our daily lives.

In "What's Inside Me, Not Mine," there is a man who drives a nail into a wall with his butt and a woman who says she's pounding a nail into the wall in front of the man. Although these two have the same role, their status is different. To a woman, a man is a wall, and the nail she is driving is the man's penis. The man's body becomes a wall and his genitals are reduced to nails. This poem causes strange laughter. The problem is that the country is a wall that explodes and is another name for history. Men are ultimately synonymous with evil habits that have been passed down from our ancestors. The satire on history is strong, and the critical insight is accurate and sharp.

Another poem, "Proof is a Dog's Thing," depicts a world that operates according to the system procedure of 'action-result-proof-cause identification', a world of mechanical functions. When a cow, a dog, and a farmer graze grass, the actions are the same, but the results are completely different. Cows eat grass, dogs spit out grass, and farmers cut the grass. We critically diagnose the world in which the result value is completely different depending on who (what) is in the position of the subject, and the world of dangerous functions in which heterogeneous results are born depending on what input is given. The prevailing view is that the world operates through accidental combinations and arrangements rather than following an inevitable order of cause and effect.

In this way, Kim Byung-ho's poetry continues to communicate with humor while going through the processes of observation, diagnosis, subversion, and reflection. Throughout his collection of poems, the poet's eyes keenly gaze at the evil and horror of reality. This point must not be missed. He is the inventor of love and the physicist of laughter who explains the shame of the corrupt modern society and the desires of modern people in a unique style.

PRAISE FOR KIM BYUNG-HO

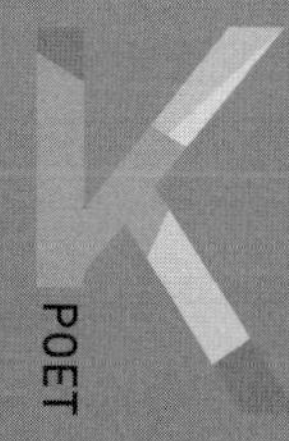

Those who know Kim Byung-ho would generally agree with the comment, "As far as I know, he is the only person in Korean literary circles who can write wonderful poetry using the 'Schrödinger equation'" (Shin Hyeong-cheol). However, this evaluation reflects only part of the literary essence he has tried to achieve. This is because his poetry does not stop at the style of scientific aesthetics, but focuses on variations of conventional literary narrative and lyricism. If you have missed the poetic tasks he paid serious attention to due to his unique 'scientific' career, this fourth collection of poems shows the results of the clear trajectory that his poetry has followed so far. This collection of poems confirms that he is a variant storyteller who has struggled not to surrender to the grammar of conventional poetry and narrative, and that he is a poet who has delved deeply into human storytelling as much as the weight of his resistance to stories allows.

His first poem, “History of Stories,” (from the collection “Slashing a Speed-bump and Lying Down” 2006) was a mythological narrative drawn in the language of symbols and connotations and an introduction pointing toward his poetic origins. The person in the poem traces the history of the story by going back to its origins, and after witnessing the shadow of the story take over the village, the poem tells how he kills Liktang, who caused it, and leaves in a hurry. Afterwards, he dismantled the conventional narratives trapped in lyrical enlightenment and brought physical equations as a tool to fully reveal the contradictions and paradoxes of life. His poetry depicts a three-dimensional narrative in which a single event forms a complex network of waves, just as Picasso showed a woman from various angles. Between the discontinuous words, the resistant particles suddenly become waves and give birth to a new story. And there, we encounter stories with various patterns that seek to "increase the freedom of the soul by looking into the bottom of existence" (from *Poetology*, 2012). In that sense, this collection of poetry appears to be a responsible result of the poetic beliefs he declared through *Poetology*.

This, when you come across an unfamiliar setting while reading his poetry, rather than being perplexed, you should look into it slowly and deeply as if you were solving the riddle called life. If you follow the heavy steps taken by such a soul, you may come across the twisted pattern of the structure of life and destiny in the density of the story. And at some point, you may gain new power to swim in this universe by lightly reciting his spell, 'Bipungchodongpalsam'.

Jo Yeongyeo (Poet)

K-POET
Love Songs Sung with the Body

Written by Kim Byung-ho
Translated by Brother Anthony of Taizé
Published by ASIA Publishers
Address 445, Hoedong-gil, Paju-si, Gyeonggi-do, Korea
(Seoul Office: 161-1, Seodal-ro, Dongjak-gu, Seoul, Korea)
Email bookasia@hanmail.net

ISBN 979-11-5662-317-5 (set) | 979-11-5662-657-2 (04810)
First published in Korea by ASIA Publishers 2023

*This book is published with the support of the Literature Translation Institute of Korea (LTI Korea).

K-Fiction series

최근에 발표된 단편소설 중 가장 우수하고 흥미로운 작품을 임신하여 출간하는 〈K-픽션〉은 한국문학의 생생한 현장을 국내외 독자들과 실시간으로 공유하고자 기획되었습니다. 원작의 재미와 품격을 최대한 살린 〈K-픽션〉 시리즈는 매 계절마다 새로운 작품을 선보입니다.

001 버핏과의 저녁 식사-**박민규** Dinner with Buffett-**Park Min-gyu**
002 아르판-**박형서** Arpan-**Park hyoung su**
003 애드벌룬-**손보미** Hot Air Balloon-**Son Bo-mi**
004 나의 클린트 이스트우드-**오한기** My Clint Eastwood-**Oh Han-ki**
005 이베리아의 전갈-**최민우** Dishonored-**Choi Min-woo**
006 양의 미래-**황정은** Kong' s Garden-**Hwang Jung-eun**
007 대니-**윤이형** Danny-**Yun I-hyeong**
008 퇴근-**천명관** Homecoming-**Cheon Myeong-kwan**
009 옥화-**금희** Ok-hwa-**Geum Hee**
010 시차-**백수린** Time Difference-**Baik Sou linne**
011 올드 맨 리버-**이장욱** Old Man River-**Lee Jang-wook**
012 권순찬과 착한 사람들-**이기호** Kwon Sun-chan and Nice People-**Lee Ki-ho**
013 알바생 자르기-**장강명** Fired-**Chang Kangmyoung**
014 어디로 가고 싶으신가요-**김애란** Where Would You Like To Go?-**Kim Ae-ran**
015 세상에서 가장 비싼 소설-**김민정** The World' s Most Expensive Novel-**Kim Min-jung**
016 체스의 모든 것-**김금희** Everything About Chess-**Kim Keum-hee**
017 할로윈-**정한아** Halloween-**Chung Han-ah**
018 그 여름-**최은영** The Summer-**Choi Eunyoung**
019 어느 피씨주의자의 종생기-**구병모** The Story of P.C.-**Gu Byeong-mo**
020 모르는 영역-**권여선** An Unknown Realm-**Kwon Yeo-sun**
021 4월의 눈-**손원평** April Snow-**Sohn Won-pyung**
022 서우-**강화길** Seo-u-**Kang Hwa-gil**
023 가출-**조남주** Run Away-**Cho Nam-joo**
024 연애의 감정학-**백영옥** How to Break Up Like a Winner-**Baek Young-ok**
025 창모-**우다영** Chang-mo-**Woo Da-young**
026 검은 방-**정지아** The Black Room-**Jeong Ji-a**
027 도쿄의 마야-**장류진** Maya in Tokyo-**Jang Ryu-jin**
028 홀리데이 홈-**편혜영** Holiday Home-**Pyun Hye-young**
029 해피 투게더-**서장원** Happy Together-**Seo Jang-won**
030 골드러시-**서수진** Gold Rush-**Seo Su-jin**
031 당신이 보고 싶어하는 세상-**장강명** The World You Want to See-**Chang Kang-Myoung**

사랑과 연애 Love and Love Affairs

21 별을 사랑하는 마음으로-**윤후명** With the Love for the Stars-**Yun Hu-myong**
22 목련공원-**이승우** Magnolia Park-**Lee Seung-u**
23 칼에 찔린 자국-**김인숙** Stab-**Kim In-suk**
24 회복하는 인간-**한강** Convalescence-**Han Kang**
25 트렁크-**정이현** In the Trunk-**Jeong Yi-hyun**

남과 북 South and North

26 판문점-**이호철** Panmunjom-**Yi Ho-chol**
27 수난 이대-**하근찬** The Suffering of Two Generations-**Ha Geun-chan**
28 분지-**남정현** Land of Excrement-**Nam Jung-hyun**
29 봄 실상사-**정도상** Spring at Silsangsa Temple-**Jeong Do-sang**
30 은행나무 사랑-**김하기** Gingko Love-**Kim Ha-kee**

바이링궐 에디션 한국 대표 소설 set 3

서울 Seoul

31 눈사람 속의 검은 항아리-**김소진** The Dark Jar within the Snowman-**Kim So-jin**
32 오후, 가로지르다-**하성란** Traversing Afternoon-**Ha Seong-nan**
33 나는 봉천동에 산다-**조경란** I Live in Bongcheon-dong-**Jo Kyung-ran**
34 그렇습니까? 기린입니다-**박민규** Is That So? I'm A Giraffe-**Park Min-gyu**
35 성탄특선-**김애란** Christmas Specials-**Kim Ae-ran**

전통 Tradition

36 무자년의 가을 사흘-**서정인** Three Days of Autumn, 1948-**Su Jung-in**
37 유자소전-**이문구** A Brief Biography of Yuja-**Yi Mun-gu**
38 향기로운 우물 이야기-**박범신** The Fragrant Well-**Park Bum-shin**
39 월행-**송기원** A Journey under the Moonlight-**Song Ki-won**
40 협죽도 그늘 아래-**성석제** In the Shade of the Oleander-**Song Sok-ze**

아방가르드 Avant-garde

41 아겔다마-**박상륭** Akeldama-**Park Sang-ryoong**
42 내 영혼의 우물-**최인석** A Well in My Soul-**Choi In-seok**
43 당신에 대해서-**이인성** On You-**Yi In-seong**
44 회색 時-**배수아** Time In Gray-**Bae Su-ah**
45 브라운 부인-**정영문** Mrs. Brown-**Jung Young-moon**

바이링궐 에디션 한국 대표 소설 set 4

디아스포라 Diaspora

46 속옷-**김남일** Underwear-Kim Nam-il
47 상하이에 두고 온 사람들-**공선옥** People I Left in Shanghai-Gong Sun-ok
48 모두에게 복된 새해-**김연수** Happy New Year to Everyone-Kim Yeon-su
49 코끼리-**김재영** The Elephant-Kim Jae-young
50 먼지별-**이경** Dust Star-Lee Kyung

가족 Family

51 혜자의 눈꽃-**천승세** Hye-ja's Snow-Flowers-Chun Seung-sei
52 아베의 가족-**전상국** Ahbe's Family-Jeon Sang-guk
53 문 앞에서-**이동하** Outside the Door-Lee Dong-ha
54 그리고, 축제-**이혜경** And Then the Festival-Lee Hye-kyung
55 봄밤-**권여선** Spring Night-Kwon Yeo-sun

유머 Humor

56 오늘의 운세-**한창훈** Today's Fortune-Han Chang-hoon
57 새-**전성태** Bird-Jeon Sung-tae
58 밀수록 다시 가까워지는-**이기호** So Far, and Yet So Near-Lee Ki-ho
59 유리방패-**김중혁** The Glass Shield-Kim Jung-hyuk
60 전당포를 찾아서-**김종광** The Pawnshop Chase-Kim Chong-kwang

바이링궐 에디션 한국 대표 소설 set 5

관계 Relationship

61 도둑견습 - **김주영** Robbery Training-Kim Joo-young
62 사랑하라, 희망 없이 - **윤영수** Love, Hopelessly-Yun Young-su
63 봄날 오후, 과부 셋 - **정지아** Spring Afternoon, Three Widows-Jeong Ji-a
64 유턴 지점에 보물지도를 묻다 - **윤성희** Burying a Treasure Map at the U-turn-Yoon Sung-hee
65 쁘이거나 쯔이거나 - **백가흠** Puy, Thuy, Whatever-Paik Ga-huim

일상의 발견 Discovering Everyday Life

66 나는 음식이다 - **오수연** I Am Food-Oh Soo-yeon
67 트럭 - **강영숙** Truck-Kang Young-sook
68 통조림 공장 - **편혜영** The Canning Factory-Pyun Hye-young
69 꽃 - **부희령** Flowers-Pu Hee-ryoung
70 피의일요일 - **윤이형** BloodySunday-Yun I-hyeong

금기와 욕망 Taboo and Desire

71 북소리 - **송영** Drumbeat-**Song Yong**
72 발칸의 장미를 내게 주었네 - **정미경** He Gave Me Roses of the Balkans-**Jung Mi-kyung**
73 아무도 돌아오지 않는 밤 - **김숨** The Night Nobody Returns Home-**Kim Soom**
74 젓가락여자 - **천운영** Chopstick Woman-**Cheon Un-yeong**
75 아직 일어나지 않은 일 - **김미월** What Has Yet to Happen-**Kim Mi-wol**

바이링궐 에디션 한국 대표 소설 set 6

운명 Fate

76 언니를 놓치다 - **이경자** Losing a Sister-**Lee Kyung-ja**
77 아들 - **윤정모** Father and Son-**Yoon Jung-mo**
78 명두 - **구효서** Relics-**Ku Hyo-seo**
79 모독 - **조세희** Insult-**Cho Se-hui**
80 화요일의 강 - **손홍규** Tuesday River-**Son Hong-gyu**

미의 사제들 Aesthetic Priests

81 고수 - **이외수** Grand Master-**Lee Oisoo**
82 말을 찾아서 - **이순원** Looking for a Horse-**Lee Soon-won**
83 상춘곡 - **윤대녕** Song of Everlasting Spring-**Youn Dae-nyeong**
84 삭매와 자미 - **김별아** Sakmae and Jami-**Kim Byeol-ah**
85 저만치 혼자서 - **김훈** Alone Over There-**Kim Hoon**

식민지의 벌거벗은 자들 The Naked in the Colony

86 감자 - **김동인** Potatoes-**Kim Tong-in**
87 운수 좋은 날 - **현진건** A Lucky Day-**Hyŏn Chin'gŏn**
88 탈출기 - **최서해** Escape-**Ch'oe So-hae**
89 과도기 - **한설야** Transition-**Han Seol-ya**
90 지하촌 - **강경애** The Underground Village-**Kang Kyŏng-ae**

바이링궐 에디션 한국 대표 소설 set 7

백치가 된 식민지 지식인 Colonial Intellectuals Turned "Idiots"

91 날개 - **이상** Wings-**Yi Sang**
92 김 강사와 T 교수 - **유진오** Lecturer Kim and Professor T-**Chin-O Yu**
93 소설가 구보씨의 일일 - **박태원** A Day in the Life of Kubo the Novelist-**Pak Taewon**
94 비 오는 길 - **최명익** Walking in the Rain-**Ch'oe Myŏngik**
95 빛 속에 - **김사량** Into the Light-**Kim Sa-ryang**